Gluten Free Christmas by KOB

Family Traditions

Copyright ©2023 by the author of this book. The book author retains sole copyright to their contributions to this book. All rights reserved.

The Family Cookbook Project provided layout designs and graphical elements are copyright Family Cookbook Project, LLC, 2023. This book was created using the FamilyCookbookProject.com software app. The book author retains sole copyright to his or her contributions to this book.

Family Cookbook Project - Helping families collect cherished recipes forever. Visit us on the Web at www.familycookbookproject.com

This book is a collection of recipes that have been passed down to me, through the years, from my family & friends. The original recipes were absolutely full of gluten! I have adjusted the recipes & revamped each one to ensure they are gluten free AND taste great as well! Thank you for all the inspiration to make them my own.

When you select your ingredients for the recipes, please read all of your labels to make sure they are gluten free!

If you do not want to make your own flour, I have found that Kinnikinnick's 1:1 blend works as a great substitute in my recipes. If you choose to use a flour, like Kinnikinnick's, make sure to read the label and if it has xanthan or guar gum in the flour then omit the xanthan gum from my recipe or it will not turn out.

I hope you enjoy my family's treasured Christmas recipes and continue traditions .. .gluten-free style!

This is the 2nd Edition of 'Gluten Free Christmas by KOB' cookbook. It has been updated with suggestions from my readers and two extra cookie recipes.

ISBN: 978-177-71375-6-4

Author and Photographer Teresa Anderson

Published and Distributed by Teresa Anderson

March 2023 (2nd Edition)

This cookbook is dedicated to my LOVE, Mike, and our children Daniel & Emily. In years to come, when you make these recipes with your own children, friends or just by yourself ... may the tastes and smells make you feel like you are 'home'.

If you have a day where the gluten free baking is not turning out 'like Mom use to make' ... CHOOSE to laugh ... then dip the cookie in a glass of milk or cup of tea ... as you don't want to waste those good ingredients! Then make sure to ENJOY the ones you love around the table. THEY are more important than what you are eating! Feel my hug and try again next time!

Plus, don't forget that I always added a secret ingredient that you did not know about ... A PINCH OF LOVE ... so just make sure to throw that in and every recipe should turn out just fine!

Love,

Teresa/Mom

p.s. Always know that you are loved.

"Be Encouraged that You CAN Bake for Christmas ... Without Gluten!"

When family and friends gather over the Christmas season, it seems like food and baking are always involved. I think our hearts know we are home for the holidays because of the tastes and smells that flow from the kitchen.

I am a celiac and once my son was also a celiac, I did not want him to lose our family traditions and tastes of home. I took dietary technology many years before celiac entered our family and it has helped with adding nutrients to my everyday baking. Although nourishing our bodies is important to me, it is not when it comes to Christmas! My Christmas cookbook's focus is on enjoying the traditions of this time of year and making the gluten free baked goods taste 'just like mom used to make'!

I have adapted my Gramma's, Mom's Sister's, Friends and Mother-in-law's old family recipes to be 'gluten-free style'. I have enjoyed revamping and changing old recipes to make them have good texture and taste great.

If you have any trouble or have questions, please check out my video classes online, I believe that some gluten free baking requires someone to SHOW you how to do it. The tips that are shown to you can make the difference of being successful.

The recipes in this book use ingredients that are easy to find in local stores. The tastes are excellent and the recipes are not complicated, YOU CAN DO IT!!!

Enjoy, Teresa

Check out online video classes or other cookbooks at

www.glutenfreeKOB.com

A Bit About Me ...

I'm a celiac and I am married to my best friend, who happens to be a dairy free type one diabetic. I am also a mom to two fabulous people. One is a celiac and the other is not (she prides her self, as being the 'normal' one in the family!). Our family has a few dietary restrictions, yet, I don't think any of us really notice…most days! It's just our 'normal'. Of course, food IS part of our daily life, but it doesn't rule our life.

I hope what I've figured out along the way can help you.

My doctor said that she believed I was a celiac since childhood, due to the damage. Yet, I had never heard the word Celiac until I was an adult. The day that I was diagnosed, my doctor scared me to death with her chat about what could happen if I continued to eat gluten. Her words stuck with me and I've never eaten gluten again!

I grew up with a dad who got up at 4 am to bake every morning, for about 50 years! He was a professional glutenated baker. When I was a child, I would walk into the bakery, and the ladies behind the counter would let me pick any mouth-watering donut I liked. Of course, I picked the biggest one I could find!

When I was first diagnosed, I really needed my doctors words in my head to keep me from eating gluten (like a soft gooey, Boston cream, donut!). Her words helped me to be able to walk away from ordering a donut with my Tim Hortons coffee. Or saying, 'no thank you' when my extended family gathered and eat cinnamon buns around the kitchen table. Or smile politely when a friend or family member made fun of my gluten-free food, never thinking that I didn't have a choice about this gluten free diet, and that this wasn't a fad diet for me. It was hard in the beginning and I appreciated my doctors fear tactic. It worked for me!

When our son was also diagnosed Celiac, I had a desire to learn how to bake gluten free. I did not want my boy to lose the taste of home. He really was my inspiration to learn!

I read a lot of books, cookbooks, blogs, I took courses, and I began to understand the chemistry behind gluten-free baking. My background in and dietary technology was also helpful and made me want to add nutrition wherever I could.

Over the years, I have adopted my grandmas, moms, sisters, friends, and mother-in-law's old family recipes to be gluten-free style! I have enjoyed revamping and changing all the new recipes to make the baked goods have excellent texture and taste. I no longer have any desire for Gluten and I have not for a long time. BUT if you are finding it hard ... I hope the recipes and tips shared help you enjoy eating baked goods again!

Bread and muffins do not have to crumble and gluten-free food does taste good! My family and I enjoy the food we eat very much.

Take the time to learn some techniques and tips, and you'll be equipped to carry on some of your old traditions gluten free style.

You can watch a video class, grab a cookbook or follow me on social media to learn some tips and bake some great foods. I hope you are successful at baking gluten free and carrying on traditions in your home,

I use ingredients that are not hard to find, the baked goods taste excellent and the recipes are not complicated, YOU CAN DO IT!

By the way, many people seem to get confused on how to say Gluten Free KOB. KOB rhymes with BOB! And KOB stands for 'Kid Okay'd Bakery'. My celiac, non celiac and their friends have okayed the baking!

Hope you join me baking online or grab a book and enjoy it as much as myself.

Enjoy!

Teresa xo

Table of Contents

Cookies 13
Squares 31
Desserts 45
Miscellaneous Christmas Recipes 59
Index by Category 81

Gluten Free
COOKIES

Chewy Gingersnap Cookies

Gluten & Dairy Free

½ cup Canola Oil
1 cup Sugar
¼ cup Molasses
1 Egg
1 tsp. Vanilla
1 ¾ cups My Favourite 1:1 GF All Purpose Flour*
2 tsps. Ginger
1 tsp. Cinnamon
1 tsp. Baking Powder
½ tsp. Xanthan Gum*
1 tsp. Baking Soda
½ tsp. Salt

*Flour blend is VERY important in end product. If you decide to use a different flour blend, do NOT add the xanthan gum from this recipe if it has a gum already in it, or it will not turn out. You will find my favourite 1:1 flour in this cookbook.

With your Kitchen-Aid or electric mixer, mix the canola oil, sugar, molasses, vanilla and egg.

In a separate bowl measure and whisk the gluten free all purpose flour blend, ginger, cinnamon, baking powder, xanthan gum, baking soda, and salt. Then add it to your wet ingredients and mix well.

Place a few tablespoons of white sugar on a plate. I use a 1 tablespoon scoop to measure the dough, and then roll it into a ball. Then dip the top of the ball of dough in the sugar.

Place the ball on a parchment lined baking sheet (with the sugar facing up).
Flatten with the palm of your hands.

Bake for 8 minutes in a 375° F oven.

You will know it is done when cracks JUST start to form on the top of the cookie. If you leave the cookies in the oven longer, they will be a very hard gingersnap.

Let the baking sheet of cookies cool on a rack before transferring them, or they will fall apart.

A Little Note: My mother-in-law made these scrumptious ginger cookies whenever we came to visit the farm. They are chewy and soft and smell just like Christmas. She made them all year, lucky for us we didn't have to wait to have them at Christmas! Our family enjoys them and thinks of her whenever I make them in our home   gluten free style!

Enjoy,
Teresa

"If you are not willing to risk the unusual, you will have to settle for the ordinary."
--Jim Rohn

Crescent Shortbread

Gluten Free

1 cup Butter
1/3 cup Sugar
1/2 cup Pecans, finely ground
1 tsp. Vanilla
Pinch of Salt
1 2/3 cups My Favourite GF Flour
1/2 tsp. Xanthan Gum

COATING
1/2 cup White Sugar
4 tsps. Cinnamon

Combine all ingredients and beat well.

Roll small pieces of dough into 'worm' shapes and then bend into crescents.

Place 1" apart on parchment lined baking sheet.

Bake for 15 - 20 minutes in a 325° F oven.

Mix the coating ingredients in a shallow bowl.

While the cookies are still warm, coat them with the cinnamon and sugar coating. Be VERY gentle as they are very fragile.

Once they cool they are easier to handle.

A Little Note: My mom made them a few times growing up and I thought they were decadent! They are very fragile ... so work very gently! They take a lot of patience due to how fragile they are. They are worth it!

Enjoy!

Sugar Cookies

Gluten & Dairy Free

2 ½ cups My Favourite 1:1 GF All Purpose Flour*
⅔ cups Sugar
½ tsp. Xanthan Gum*
½ tsp. Salt
1 tsp. Vanilla
2 Eggs
1 cup Hard Block Margarine, I use Parkay

*Flour blend is VERY important in end product. If you decide to use a different flour blend, do NOT add the xanthan gum from this recipe if it has a gum already in it, or it will not turn out. My favourite 1:1 flour is in this book.

In a bowl, whisk the flour, sugar, and xanthan gum.

With an electric mixer, beat the softened margarine and sugar until creamed.

Beat in the eggs and vanilla. Slowly add the dry ingredients. Beat the dough until it is well combined and sticks together.

On a lightly floured pastry mat, roll out small portions of dough at a time. I use a handy rolling pin that has rings on the end that allows me to roll dough evenly, I find it works really well.

With a highly floured cookie cutter, cut dough into desired shapes. Be careful transferring shapes to a parchment lined baking sheet.

Bake for eight minutes in a 350° F oven.

You will know the cookies are done when the edges are just turning golden.

Let the cookies cool completely on sheets, or they will crumble. Transfer to a cooling rack and then decorate when you are ready.

These cookies freeze well. I often make them ahead and then bring them out to decorate when I have time. The decorated cookies can be put back into the freezer and then taken out when needed.

I like to decorate sugar cookies with royal icing. I have two royal icing recipes in this book, use the one that is for sugar cookies and have fun!

A Little Note: I have made sugar cookies since my kids were little. Sugar cookies really are a hit on a Christmas baking plate.

Our family still sits around the table one evening and spends hours decorating Christmas cookies together. One of my favourite family traditions!

Enjoy,
Teresa

"We must risk going too far to discover just how far we can go."
--Jim Rohn

Royal Icing for Sugar Cookies

Gluten & Dairy Free

1 kg. Icing Sugar
5 tbsps. Meringue Powder*
½ to ¾ cup Warm Water
2 tsps. Vanilla Extract (or flavour of your choice ... make sure oil free)

*Meringue Powder can be hard to find gluten free. I have found some online or in my local Bulk Barn (sealed bag).

Stir the icing sugar and meringue powder in a mixing bowl.

In a glass measuring cup stir the flavour into the warm water.

Turn the Kitchen-Aid or electric mixer on the lowest setting and slowly add the water mixture to the icing sugar mixture. The icing will become thick.

Continue to add the water until it becomes a honey consistency. Then stop adding water and mix on medium speed for 2 minutes. The icing will become thick and fluffy.

When you are piping around the edge of a cookie, the icing should be the consistency of toothpaste.

The flooding consistency should be like shower liquid soap.

Just add a 1/4 teaspoon of water at a time to reach proper consistency. It doesn't take much water to change how thick the icing is, so add water slowly!

You can put icing into sandwich or decorating bags to decorate the cookies. It makes it easy to decorate with less mess!

A Little Note: I LOVE decorating sugar cookies! Let the cookies sit for a couple of hours on wax paper. Then freeze. My brother-in-law doesn't love gluten free goodies, but one thing that touched my heart is that he really likes my decorated gluten free sugar cookies .. that is a huge compliment!

*Enjoy,
Teresa*

"Do the right thing. Do it right. Do it right now."
--Unknown

Great Gramma Swansons Shortbread

Gluten Free

1 cup Butter
1/2 cup Brown Sugar
1 Egg Yolk
1 tsp. Vanilla
2 cups My Favourite GF 1:1 Flour

Cream first four ingredients until fluffy in Kitchen-Aide.

Add the flour slowly and mix until well combined.

Roll out 1/4" thick and cut into shapes or put into a pie plate and cut into wedges after it has baked.

Preheat oven to 300° F.

If you have rolled out cookies they will take 15-18 minutes to bake.

If you have put into a pie plate it will take about 30 minutes to bake (remember to cut into wedges after done baking!).

A Little Note: I never had these cookie from my Great Gramma Swanson, yet I was giving the recipe and told that she made them for years. She was from England and I imagine that she would have one with a cup of tea!

Enjoy!

"In the middle of difficulty lies opportunity."
--Albert Einstein

Gingerbread House & Gingerbread Men

Gluten & Dairy Free

1 ¼ tbsps. Xanthan Gum
1 ½ tbsps. Baking Powder
1 tbsp. Epicure's Gingerbread Spice Mix
1 ½ cups Icing Sugar
1 cup Brown Sugar
1 cup Hard Margarine (I use Parkay)
4 Eggs
½ cup Dark Molasses
1 tsp. Salt
¼ cup Sorghum Flour
½ cup Amaranth Flour
1 cup Potato Starch
1 ¼ cups White Rice Flour
1 ½ cups Brown Rice Flour

In a large bowl, mix together the flours, starch, xanthan gum, baking powder, salt and spices until well combined. Set aside. In another bowl, cream together the margarine, icing sugar, brown sugar, eggs, and molasses. This is big batch of dough, I normally use my Kitchen-Aid to mix it. Slowly add flour mixture to the margarine mixture, until well combined.

Roll the dough on a floured pastry mat. I like my cookies and house fairly thin and uniform and therefore use my rolling pin with the 1/4 inch circle. This allows every wall/roof to be exactly 1/4 inch thick which helps with building and baking. I use a handy rolling pin that has rings on the end that allows me to roll dough evenly, I find it works really well.

Use a template or cutters to cut out the house pieces and/or gingerbread men.

I actually make gingerbread families ... I have a man, woman, boy, girl, cat and dog ...as that works for my family. It's kinda fun! You could get cutters that work for your family.

Use a flipper to pick up cut out shapes and place on parchment lined baking sheets. Place shapes that are similarly sized on same sheets so baking time will work out per sheet.

I bake my gingerbread men for about 12 minutes and my

gingerbread walls for 15+ minutes in at 350° F oven.

You will know they are done when the corners of the cookies start to brown. I take them out of the oven when they JUST start to brown ... as they are still a bit soft. If you like them snappier in texture, just leave them in the oven another minute or two.

For the walls, you do not want them soft, as they need to be sturdy!

A Little Note: We have made a gingerbread house and gingerbread families with our kids every year. When they were smaller, we got together with cousins and made miniature houses as well.

This recipe is just like the cookies I made with my family for years. You can use the dough for a gingerbread-house and gingerbread-men.

When the kids were small I would read the storybook about the gingerbread man getting out of the oven and running around ... then as the gingerbread was in the oven they would peer through the glass hoping one would jump out. They had such anticipation. Gingerbread cookies were pretty fun around our house!

I'm so glad we can continue traditions .. gluten free style!

Use the Royal Icing for Gingerbread, to hold your gingerbread house together and to decorate it. If you are making gingerbread-men, I would use the Sugar Cookie Royal Icing as it is not as hard and tastes better.

Enjoy,
Teresa

"I am always doing things I can't do, that's how I get to do them."
--Picasso

Royal Icing for Gingerbread House

Gluten & Dairy Free

4 cups Icing Sugar
2 tbsps. Meringue Powder*
6 tbsps. Warm Water

*Meringue Powder can be hard to find gluten free. I have found some online or in my local Bulk Barn (sealed bag).

Put all of the above ingredients into your mixing bowl, I use my Kitchen-Aid. SLOWLY turn on beater, or it will splash all over you!

Turn timer on and beat for 7 minutes. The texture changes as it beats. Best to use it right away to build your gingerbread house.

Put icing into a piping bag or a ziplock bag and then cut a little hole in the corner and use it to pipe icing on the edges of 'walls' and 'roof' to attach the walls and roof together. The icing dries hard and will hold your walls and roof together very well. I often join the walls and roof earlier in the day and let it set before my family decorates.

This icing is best used right away. If you are making it ahead, like myself, then put a wet tea towel on top of the bowl to avoid the icing drying out and hardening. You may need to add a drop or two of water to thin it out if you use it a couple of hours later.

A Little Note: Since our kids were small we have always made a gingerbread house. It was easier to do when we could buy the little kits in the grocery store. Yet, I believe becoming a celiac should not change traditions ... we just need to change how we do it! There are four in my family and we all take a side of the house and decorate at the same time with carols playing in the background. I put icing in a decorating bag or sandwich bag (with a hole cut out of the corner) for each person and then we attach as much candy as we can. My husband loves making fences with GF pretzels ... have fun creating memories!

Enjoy,
Teresa

"When you know what you want, and you want it badly enough, you'll find a way to get it"
--Jim Rohn

Whipped Shortbread

Gluten & Egg Free

1 cup Butter
½ cup Icing Sugar
1 tsp. Vanilla
2 cups My Favourite 1:1 GF All
   Purpose Flour*
1 tsp. Xanthan Gum*

Maraschino Cherries or Sprinkles
   (optional)

*Flour blend is VERY important in end product. If you decide to use a different flour blend, do NOT add the xanthan gum from this recipe if it has a gum already in it, or it will not turn out. You will find my favourite 1:1 flour recipe in this book.

Beat the butter for 5 minutes in your Kitchen-Aid or electric mixer. Set a timer, as this is how the cookies will melt in your mouth! Add icing sugar and vanilla. Beat until smooth. Whisk the flour and Xanthum Gum then slowly add it into the butter mixture.

TWO options of what to do with dough;

The FIRST option;

The first option is to use a small scoop to make 1" balls of dough. Place the balls on a parchment lined cookie sheet. Dough will be soft. Flatten balls with a fork that has been dipped in icing sugar. Place a 1/4 piece of maraschino cherry in the centre of each cookie (this is optional) ... but it makes the cookies look very pretty!

The SECOND option:

The second option is to divide the dough in half. Roll each half into two logs, approximately 1.5 to 2 inches in diameter. Pour sprinkles onto waxed paper and roll each log in the sprinkles, covering the outside of the logs completely. Then, use a sharp knife and slice cookies ¼ to ½ inch thick. Place slices onto a parchment lined cookie sheet.

For both options, bake at 325° F for approximately 15 minutes or until the bottoms begin to brown slightly.

Let the cookies cool completely on the baking sheet before removing them, as they will crumble into a million pieces if you do not wait.

These cookies freeze well. I have been known to eat one frozen .. and they taste great.

A Little Note: My Mom always made LOTS of shortbread throughout the years. Her shortbread literally melts in your mouth. She has always said the trick to having mouth-watering shortbread is beating your butter for at least 5 minutes or longer. So, take advice from my Mom and enjoy her mouth-watering shortbread recipe ... gluten free style!

Enjoy,
Teresa

"The future belongs to those who believe in the beauty of their dreams."
--Eleanor Roosevelt

Another Great Recipe: _____

Ingredients: *Directions:*

Tips:

Another Great Recipe: _____

Ingredients: *Directions:*

_____   _____
_____   _____
_____   _____
_____   _____
_____   _____
_____   _____
_____   _____
_____   _____
_____   _____
_____   _____
_____   _____
_____   _____
_____   _____
_____   _____
_____   _____
_____   _____
_____   _____
_____   _____
_____   _____
_____   _____
_____   _____
_____   _____
_____   _____
_____   _____

Tips:

_____
_____
_____
_____

Gluten Free
SQUARES

Chocolate Dreams

Gluten Free

⅔ cup Butter
½ cup White Sugar
½ cup Brown Sugar
2 tsps. Baking Powder
1 tsp. Xanthan Gum*
½ tsp. Salt
½ cup Walnuts
2 ½ cups My Favourite 1:1 GF All
  Purpose Flour*
1 tsp. Vanilla
2 cups Chocolate Chips
4 Egg Yolks

TOPPING
4 Egg Whites
1 cup Brown Sugar

*Flour blend is VERY important in end product. If you decide to use a different flour blend, do NOT add the xanthan gum from this recipe if it has a gum already in it, or it will not turn out. My favourite 1:1 flour is in this cookbook.

With your Kitchen-Aid or electric mixer, cream together the butter, white sugar, brown sugar, egg yolks and vanilla. Scrape sides of bowl and beat well.

Whisk flour, salt, xanthan gum and baking powder in a bowl. Then add these dry ingredients to the butter mixture. Beat well and then spread this mixture on the bottom of a 9x13" greased pan, press into pan with the palm of your hand.

Sprinkle chocolate chips and walnuts on top.
My husband said that his mom didn't add the walnuts … you can omit if you choose…. But not the chocolate!

TOPPING
Beat egg whites until stiff. With a spatula, fold the brown sugar into the beaten egg whites. Spread evenly over chocolate chip and walnut mixture.

Bake 30-40 minutes in a 350° F oven.

Meringue should be slightly brown.

Let the squares cool completely. Then cut carefully with a sharp knife. The meringue can break and crack when cutting. I have found dipping a knife in hot water can help with the process.

A Little Note: My mother-in-law's recipe has been transformed into a gluten free dream. Our girl loves them! They are easy to make ahead and keep well in the freezer.

Enjoy,
Teresa

"Some dream of doing great things, while others stay awake and get on with it."
--Unknown

Nanaimo Bars

Gluten Free

BOTTOM LAYER
½ cup Butter, cut into pieces
¼ cup Sugar
5 tbsps. Cocoa Powder
1 large Egg
1 ¾ cups Gluten Free Graham
  Crackers, crushed
½ cup Walnuts, finely chopped
1 cup Coconut, shredded

MIDDLE LAYER
½ cup Butter
3 tbsps. Whipping Cream, not
  whipped!
2 tbsps. Bird's Custard Powder
1 ½ cups Icing Sugar

TOP LAYER
4 oz. Semi-Sweet Chocolate,
  coarsely chopped
2 tbsps. Butter

Grease an 8x8 inch cake pan.

I put a piece of parchment on the bottom of the pan with the sides coming up over the edge ... this makes it easy to lift the squares out to cut.

BOTTOM LAYER

Melt butter in a saucepan. Remove from heat and mix in the sugar and cocoa. While stirring, slowly add the egg. Stir quickly so you do not scramble the egg. Return the pan to the stove on medium heat and cook until mixture has just thickened. Take pan off the heat and stir in the gluten free graham crumbs, walnuts, and coconut. Press this mixture into the bottom of the prepared 8X8 pan. Set to the side.

MIDDLE LAYER

In your electric mixer, add Bird's Custard powder, icing sugar, butter and cream. Beat for 2-3 minutes. Spread mixture evenly over the COMPLETELY cooled bottom layer.

TOP LAYER

Melt the chocolate with butter in the microwave, stir every 10 seconds until smooth. Quickly spread chocolate mixture over middle layer, spread evenly. Chill until chocolate has hardened. Cut into squares. These squares freeze and defrost nicely.

A Little Note: My husband, son and mom are the biggest fans of Nanaimo Bars. Truthfully, they are not my favourite. Yet, I make them for the ones I love. They are definitely a Christmas Tradition for many.

Enjoy,
Teresa

"We all need lots of powerful long range goals to help us past the short term obstacles."
--Jim Rohn

Toffee Bars

Gluten & Egg Free

¾ cup Butter, softened
½ cup Sugar
1 ½ cups My Favourite 1:1 GF All Purpose Flour*
1 tsp. xanthan gum*
½ cup Butter (Dairy Free, if needed)
¼ cup Sugar
2 tbsp. Corn syrup
⅔ cup Sweetened Condensed Milk
8 oz. Semi Sweet Chocolate

Hope You Enjoy Making Family Traditions ~ Love ~ From My Family

*Flour blend is VERY important in end product. If you decide to use a different flour blend, do NOT add the xanthan gum from this recipe if it has a gum already in it, or it will not turn out. My favourite 1:1 flour is in this cookbook.

Cream the 3/4 cup softened butter and the first amount of sugar with a Kitchen-Aid or electric mixer. Slowly add flour and xanthan gum, until well combined. Press dough into an 8x8 inch pan. Bake in 350° F oven until brown, approximately 20-25 minutes.

While the cookie layer bakes, make your toffee centre.

In a heavy pan, place the 1/2 cup butter, second amount of sugar, corn syrup, and sweetened condensed milk. Then cook over medium heat, stirring constantly … really! Don't stop as it burns quickly. Once it comes to a boil, turn heat to low and continue to stir for 10 minutes or until it changes color (slightly golden color).

Once it has cooled down a bit, pour over baked shortbread crust. Let both layers cool.

In a glass bowl, melt eight ounces of semi sweet chocolate in the microwave. Stir. Once smooth, pour evenly over the toffee mixture.

Place pan into the fridge. Let it cool completely before cutting. Cut and then place pieces in a container to freeze. Put wax paper in between layers. Take out pieces throughout the Christmas Season to add to a plate of Christmas goodies.

A Little Note: When I married my husband, over 20 years ago, he introduced me to these squares. In our first little apartment's kitchen, we made these together. We have never missed a year since then! His mom made them for Christmas, and to him, it would not be Christmas with out them. They are very sweet, but we cut them small, freeze them and enjoy one slice from the freezer at a time. Be patient making the toffee, it takes time ...and a lot of stirring!

Enjoy,
Teresa

"If you go to work on your goals, your goals will go to work on you. If you go to work on your plan, your plan will go to work on you. Whatever good things we build end up building us."
--Jim Rohn

Date Squares

Gluten, Dairy & Egg Free

CRUST
½ cup Brown Rice Flour
2 tbsp. Millet Flour
2 tbsp. Sorghum Flour
2 tbsp. Amaranth Flour
2 tbsp. White Rice Flour
1 cup Gluten Free Oats
¼ cup Brown Sugar
½ cup Butter
1 tsp. Vanilla

FILLING
650 grams Dates, chopped
1 cup Water
¼ cup Orange Juice

Make sure your dates are pitted. Then put chopped dates and water into saucepan. Cook on medium heat for 6 to 8 minutes, stirring constantly. Remove from heat and stir in the orange juice. Set to the side.

In a mixing bowl, add the brown rice flour, millet flour, sorghum flour, amaranth flour, white rice flour, gluten free oats and brown sugar. Stir to ensure well combined. Then add cut up butter and vanilla to dry ingredients. Rub mixture back and forth in your hands until crumbly and evenly combined.

Place 2/3 of the crumbled mixture into the bottom of a greased 8x8 pan. Press this mixture down, evenly, with palm of your hand.

Then spread date filling evenly on top of crumble mixture.

Sprinkle the remaining crumb mixture over the dates and then lightly press with the palm of your hand.

Bake date squares in a 350° F oven for 20-25 minutes.

You will be able to tell it's done when the edges are getting a bit brown.

Let it cool completely, or they will be very soft and hard to handle.

Cut into squares. I keep them in the freezer, with wax paper between the layers. Cut them ahead and separate them, this makes it easy to grab a few for a Christmas baking tray.

A Little Note: My Gramma always had date squares on her Christmas baking list. Date squares are a treat that I have always loved. I add many different gluten free grains to the squares to increase nutrients, fibre and flavour. My non-celiac sister absolutely loves this recipe, she even makes it with all the unique gluten free grains instead of 'normal' flour ... she says it's better!

Enjoy,
Teresa

"Goals... There's no telling what you can do when you get inspired by them. There's no telling what you can do when you believe in them. There's no telling what will happen when you act upon them."
--Jim Rohn

Pineapple Squares

Gluten & Dairy Free

BASE
1 ¼ cups My Favourite 1:1 GF All Purpose Flour*
130 grams Butter (use dairy free, if needed)
¼ cup Sugar
1 tsp. Xanthan Gum*

TOPPING
14 grams Butter (use dairy free, if needed)
½ cup Sugar
1 Egg
14 oz can Crushed Pineapple
½ cup Flaked Coconut (separated in half)

*Flour blend is VERY important in end product. If you decide to use a different flour blend, do NOT add the xanthan gum from this recipe if it has a gum already in it, or it will not turn out. My favourite 1:1 flour is in this cookbook.

Before you start, open your can of pineapple and empty it into a sieve, and let it drain as you prepare the squares. Once in a while take a spoon, or your hand, and push on the pineapple to try to get rid of excess liquid.

BASE

Grate the butter. In a medium bowl, whisk the flour, sugar and xanthan gum together. Then add the grated butter. Stir with a spoon. Pat down into 8x8 inch ungreased pan.
Bake for 15 minutes in a 350° F oven.

TOPPING

While the base is in the oven, prepare the topping. Cream together the butter, sugar and egg. Use a spoon to fold in the well-drained pineapple and 1/4 cup coconut. Mix well. Spread this pineapple mixture evenly over the baked base, sprinkle 1/4 cup coconut over the top. Return the pineapple squares to the oven and bake for 20-25 minutes. Let them cool completely before cutting.

I keep these squares in the freezer, as they defrost quickly. I cut into squares and then put wax paper between the layers. They are great to add to a Christmas baking tray.

A Little Note: My mom made pineapple squares when I was growing up. Once I was diagnosed celiac, she never made them again. My children had never had pineapple squares. In 2020, my sister made some gluten free pineapple squares. They loved them so much that they actually were hiding in her boot-room with her …. hoping I would not see them eating the squares before dinner! As they all came into the kitchen, they were wiping the crumbs off their face trying to look innocent. So, I HAD to get her recipe and include it in our family book. Hopefully you enjoy these squares, as much as my kids! I did change a thing or two … so her's will always be THEE BEST to my kids!

Enjoy,
Teresa

"Obstacles are those frightful things you see when you take your eyes off your goal."
--Henry Ford

Another Great Recipe: _____

Ingredients: *Directions:*

Tips:

Another Great Recipe: _____

Ingredients: Directions:

Gluten Free
DESSERTS

Butter Tart Filling

Gluten Free

1 cup Brown Sugar
1 cup Raisins
2 Eggs
1 ½ tsps. Vanilla
¼ cup Cream
½ cup Pecans, chopped
⅓ cup Butter

In a saucepan, add the butter, sugar, raisins, eggs, vanilla and cream. Mix and bring to a boil, stirring constantly. Take off the heat. Add pecans and stir well.

Fill tart shells with butter tart filling. Your tart shells can be bought or homemade. I have included my pie crust recipe in this cookbook, if you would like to make your own.

Bake filled tart shells for 15 minutes at 350° F. Cool completely before serving. These tarts freeze well.

A Little Note: At Christmas, my mom loves butter tarts. When I was a kid, she would line our counters with fresh tarts. Whether you make or buy your tart shells, I hope you enjoy butter tarts as much as my mom!

Enjoy,
Teresa

"Never begin the day until it's finished on paper."
--Jim Rohn

Pumpkin Pie Filling

Gluten Free

3 Eggs
2 cups Pumpkin Purée
½ cup Brown Sugar
½ cup Whipped Cream
1 tsp. Cinnamon
½ tsp. Ginger
¼ tsp. Cloves
Pecans (optional)
Whipped Cream for topping the pie
  (optional)

Place all of the ingredients, other than pecans, into a mixing bowl. I use Kitchen-Aid or electric mixer to beat the ingredients for 2 minutes. Scrape the bowl with a spatula and then beat for another minute.

Fill the pie shell with the pumpkin pie filling. Your pie shell can be bought or homemade. I think homemade is always tastier! I have included my pie crust recipe in this cookbook.

You have a few options for the top of your pie;
1. Leave the pie plain
2. Cut extra pie dough with small cookie cutters and decorate the top of the pie
3. Sprinkle top of pie with pecans
4. Candy pecans and then put on top of pie

Bake the pie at 400° F for 15 minutes.

Then turn your oven down to 350°F and bake for 30-40 minutes.

The timing will depend on how deep you have made your pie. Take it out of the oven when you first start to see some cracks on the outer inch of pie filling.

Then let it cool completely before you serve.

We like to serve each piece with fresh whipped cream. I often sweeten my cream with a bit of maple syrup instead of sugar, it tastes nice with the pumpkin.

A Little Note: As for me, I could eat Pumpkin Pie anytime of the year!

When I grew up, we always had pumpkin pie for Christmas Dinner. Now, my in-laws and my family make trifle. I didn't know that families were 'allowed' to change traditions?!?!?

Don't tell my family, but I secretly prefer pumpkin pie! Whether you make or buy your pie shells, I hope you enjoy this pumpkin pie filling!

*Enjoy,
Teresa*

"Formal education will make you a living. Self-education will make you a fortune."
--Jim Rohn

Pie Dough

Gluten & Dairy Free

75 grams Hard Margarine (I use Parkay)
75 grams Butter (Use Dairy Free, if needed)
2 cups My Favourite 1:1 GF Flour*
½ tsp. Salt
½ tsp. Sugar
1 tsp. Vinegar
1 Large Egg
⅓ cup Cold Water

*Flour blend is VERY important in end product. My favourite 1:1 flour is in this cookbook.

Measure the flour, sugar and salt into a mixing bowl. Whisk. Weigh the butter and margarine and grate into flour mixture. Then stir with a spoon.

Add the vinegar, egg and cold water to the mixing bowl. With a Kitchen-Aid or electric mixer, beat for approximately 2 minutes. The mixture should not have any dry or crumbly bits.

Roll your dough out to 1/8 inch thickness and place into a pie plate or tart shell.

I use a handy rolling pin that has rings on the end that allows me to roll dough evenly, I find it works really well ... but there is no problem at all to roll the dough out and estimate. I just find this rolling pin makes the job easier.

You may bake the shell and store it in the freezer for later use or fill the pie shell with a filling of your choice and bake.

In this recipe book I have included pumpkin pie filling and butter tart filing, if you are interested to try.

If you have made a fruit pie, bake for 10 minutes at 400°F and then turn down the oven to 350°F and bake for an additional 20 minutes.

You will know the pie is done when the fruit starts to bubble.

A Little Note: I grew up eating pie. My dad was a professional baker, and loved pie! My mom also loved pie and she was taught how to make pie by my Gramma who made the BEST pear pie. My mom made pie for every occasion, she is actually the BEST pie baker that I know! The only issue is that she makes pie with gluten. Once celiac hit, I had to figure out how to make gluten free pie. NOW, that was not easy! There was a lot of crumbled messes and crusts that were rock hard. Finally I have the perfect crust and it always turns out.

Enjoy,
Teresa

"You don't get paid for the hour. You get paid for the value you bring to the hour."
--Jim Rohn

Sticky Toffee Pudding

Gluten Free

225 grams Dates, chopped finely
1 cup Boiling Water
½ cup Butter, room temperature
1 cup Brown Sugar
4 Eggs
1 ¾ cups My Favourite 1:1 GF Flour*
1 tsp. Baking Powder
1 tsp. Xanthan Gum*
1 tsp. Baking Soda
2 tbsp. Instant Coffee Granules

TOFFEE SAUCE
1 cup Butter
1 ¾ cups Brown Sugar
⅔ cups Whipping Cream

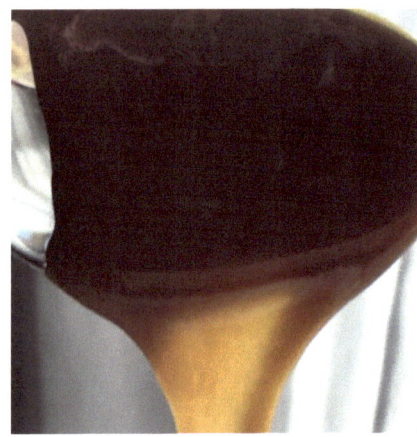

*Flour blend is VERY important in end product. If you decide to use a different flour blend, do NOT add the xanthan gum from this recipe if it has a gum already in it, or it will not turn out. My Favourite GF Flour recipe is in this cookbook.

Place the dates in a bowl. Pour the boiling water over the dates and let cool for approximately 1 hour.

Cream butter and sugar. Add 2 eggs, one egg at a time, beating well after each addition. Whisk the flour, xanthan gum and baking powder. Add half of the flour mixture to the butter mixture, blend well. Add remaining 2 eggs, 1 at a time, beating well after each addition. Add remaining flour and beat well. Combine baking soda, coffee and dates. Add to dough and beat well. Pour batter into greased muffin tins, fill 1/2 to 2/3 full. Makes about a dozen regular sized muffin size cakes.
Bake for 18-20 minutes in a 350° F oven.

These little cakes can be made earlier in the day and then just pour warm toffee sauce over the mini cakes before serving ... with a bit of whipped cream.

TOFFEE SAUCE

Place the butter, brown sugar and whipping cream in a sauce pan. Stir constantly over medium heat, once it boils turn down the heat to a simmer and stir for 15 minutes or until it thickens.

I usually make the toffee a couple of hours before supper, as it will thicken as it cools. Then I just warm it up before serving. Serve each person a mini cake in a bowl or plate, pour this warm toffee sauce on-top and add a bit of cream on the very top.

A Little Note: Many years ago, a friend gave me this recipe. It was full of gluten, but I have changed it to be gluten free. I make it once during the Christmas Season, as it is very sweet. The warm homemade toffee poured over the cake and then topped with fresh whipped cream, is heaven in a bowl.

Enjoy,
Teresa

"There are two kinds of people, those who do the work and those who take the credit. Try to be in the first group - there is less competition."
--Indira Ghandi

Trifle

Gluten Free

Gluten Free Cake or Cupcakes of Your Choice (homemade or store bought .. what ever you like)
¼ cup Whipped Cream
1 can (540 ml) Canned Cherry Pie Filling
1 Gluten Free Chocolate Bar

MOM'S CUSTARD
2 cups Milk
2 ½ tbsps. Cornstarch
¼ cup Sugar
2 Eggs, yolks only
½ tsp. Vanilla
1 tbsp. Butter

If you are hosting Christmas or responsible for the dessert, then put all the layers of this trifle into a large, beautiful glass bowl.

My celiac son loves trifle yet can not eat it at my in-laws or his aunts house due to gluten. Therefore, I decided to make individual gluten free trifle in sealer jars. I top each jar with a lid or wax paper and a ribbon. The trifle can be easily taken to any house for Christmas dinner. A great way to join in traditions.

Make the pudding first so that it can cool.
In a saucepan, place the milk and sugar. Heat the milk mixture on medium heat, stirring constantly. Add a bit of the milk mixture to a small bowl with the cornstarch and then whisk into the milk in the saucepan. In a separate bowl, add the warm milk mixture to the eggs (stir quickly as you do not want to cook your egg). Then add the egg mixture to the saucepan. Continue to stir until the milk has bubbles and starts to thicken. Set to the side, to cool.

You can use any cake you would like for the trifle. If I have time, I bake a cake from scratch and if not, I use a gluten free cake mix.

Cut the cake into medium sized chunks. Set some chunks of cake in the bottom of the jar to cover the bottom or the bottom of a glass bowl. Then spoon the cherries over the cake. Then spoon the cooled pudding over the cherries. Repeat the layers as many times as you can.

Just before you serve the trifle, top it with whipped cream.

I think it looks nice to have chocolate curls on the top. Simply take a vegetable peeler and push down (slowly and steadily) along the length of a chunk of chocolate, and you will have beautiful curls. Sprinkle the curls on top of the whipped cream.

A Little Note: My Aunty and mother-in-law both made trifle for Christmas Dinner. They both made it very different, and both were wonderful! My mom-in-law made it with cake, jello, fruit cocktail, Bird's Custard and cream. My sisters-in-law love to eat the leftovers for Boxing Day breakfast. Really, if you put any cake, pudding, fruit and cream in a bowl .. it is good!

Enjoy,
Teresa

"Income seldom exceeds personal development."
--Jim Rohn

*Another Great Recipe:*_____

Ingredients: *Directions:*

Tips:

Another Great Recipe: _____

Ingredients: Directions:

Tips:

Gluten Free
MISC.

Boxing Day Dip

Gluten Free

1 package of Cream Cheese (8 oz)
½ cup Mayonnaise
7 drops Franks Hot Sauce (or hot sauce of your choice)
¼ tsp. Garlic Salt
1 can Artichokes, drained and chopped
2 cups Cheddar Cheese, grated
¼ to ⅓ cup Cherry Tomatoes, quartered
3 Green Onions, finely chopped

With your electric mixer, beat mayonnaise, cream cheese, hot sauce, and garlic salt. Beat until smooth. Then mix in 1 3/4 cup cheese and artichokes.

Spread creamy mixture into pie plate.

Sprinkle with green onions, tomatoes and remaining 1/4 cup cheese.

Bake 15 to 20 minutes at 375 ° F.

You will know the dip is done when it has started to bubble and has browned slightly on the edges. Serve warm with Tostitos or gluten free crackers.

A Little Note: My sister has made this dip for years. My son loves it so very much! It goes well with a games night with cousins and extended family!

You can make it earlier in the day and then just throw it in the oven when you are ready to play games!

Enjoy,
Teresa

My Favourite 1:1 Gluten Free Flour

Gluten, Dairy & Egg Free

294 grams White Rice Flour
92 grams Brown Rice Flour
86 grams Potato Starch
37 grams Tapioca Starch

Ensure all of your flours and starches are gluten free and ground on a gluten free mill.
Use a kitchen scale to measure your ingredients. Stir well using a spoon and a whisk. Then place in an airtight container to keep your flour fresh. Remember to whisk your flour each time you use it to ensure it is well mixed. Due to the different flours and starches they can separate out while in the container. This flour does not have xanthan gum in it, which I like because you do not always need xanthan gum in every recipe. Remember you may need to add xanthan gum to recipes to make them turn out, I usually add 1/2 to 1 teaspoon per cup.

A Little Note: Gluten Free flour makes or breaks your recipe. I have tested all of my recipes with other 1:1 store bought flour blends and each one will make the recipe turn out different. This blend truly makes baked goods taste great and have wonderful texture. I don't love weighing and making flour, but if you make a container ahead then you are ready to bake when you feel like it.

Enjoy, Teresa

Chex Mix - Nut and Bolts

Gluten & Dairy Free

9 cups Rice Chex Cereal
3 cups Honey Chex Cereal
8 cups Pretzels (Snyders has Gluten Free!)
2 ½ cups Mixed Nuts (make sure gluten free!)
4 cups Whole O's (Nature's Path)

SAUCE
2 cups Butter (Dairy Free, if needed)
1 tbsp. Seasoning Salt
½ tsp. Onion Powder
3 tbsps. Worcestershire Sauce (French's Brand is gluten free)
2 tbsps. Garlic Powder
1 tbsp. Paprika

Preheat oven to 250°F.

You will need a large roaster to hold all the ingredients. Place all of the dry ingredients into roaster and stir.

Over medium heat, melt butter. Then mix in the remainder of the sauce ingredients. Pour the sauce over the dry ingredients and mix well, stir gently.

Bake in the oven for 2 hours, stir gently every 30 minutes. The butter mixture will absorb, and the mixture will get dry. It will smell wonderful, and it tastes pretty good warm! Let it cool. I put it into a sealed container and place in my freezer. Then, I take it out one bowl at a time. It stays tasting fresh and does not get stale.

A Little Note: You can substitute cereals for ones that you find locally. My family all helps make this recipe. It is not hard and doesn't require 4 people, but it is tradition and fun to get in the kitchen and make it together.

Enjoy,
Teresa

Sweet Potatoes

Gluten, Dairy & Egg Free

2 to 3 Sweet Potatoes, medium
2 tbsps. Butter (you can substitute Dairy Free, if needed)
2-3 tbsps. Brown Sugar
1 tsp. Cinnamon
¼ cup Pecans, coarsely chopped

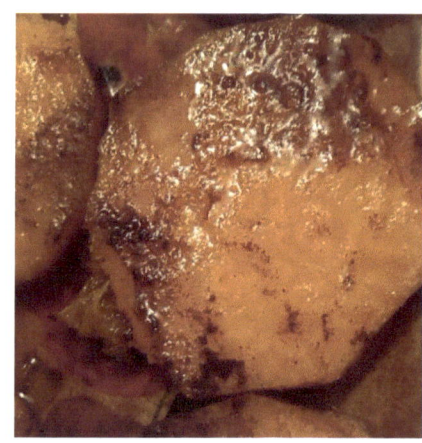

Peel the sweet potatoes. Cut the sweet potatoes into 1 to 1 1/2 inch circles.

Place the circles into a large shallow casserole dish (ideal single layered).

Cut the butter into small chunks and place evenly all over the sweet potatoes.

Sprinkle the tops of the sweet potatoes evenly with the brown sugar and cinnamon. Coarsely chop the pecans & then sprinkle on top.

Bake in a 375° F oven for 1 hour.

I like this dish because it is forgiving. If supper is delayed, they keep well in a warm oven. If your oven needs to be a bit higher or lower for a different dish … these will still turn out (within reason!).

You can also make these ahead, just boil the sweet potato circles for 5 minutes, place in ice water to cool and then place in the pan with butter, sugar, cinnamon and pecans.

Cover and place sweet potatoes in the fridge and they are ready when you are! If you do this, they will need longer to bake being so cold from the fridge.

A Little Note: My Mom made this dish, every year. I think that I love these sweet potatoes more than the turkey! She added triple the amount of butter and sugar than I do, so how could it not taste heavenly!

To me, this is a must around the Christmas dinner table.

Enjoy,
Teresa

"Without a sense of urgency, desire loses its value."
--Jim Rohn

Fruit Compôte

Gluten, Dairy & Egg Free

½ cup Dried Apricots
½ cup Dried Apples
½ cup Dried Prunes
¼ cup Dried Figs
2 tbsps. Craisins
2 tbsps. Raisins
3 slices Lemon
3 sticks Cinnamon
¾ cup Apple Juice
1 ¼ cups Water

Make sure that the dried fruit is gluten free. It is pretty common to have wheat in packaged dried fruit, so just check your labels!

Place all of the ingredients into a large pot. Over medium high heat bring to a boil and then turn down to low and simmer for 30 minutes or until soft. Take the pot off the heat and eat warm or cool. Let it cool completely, before you put into the fridge. Place the fruit compôte into a container that seals and it will keep well in the fridge for a week.
Take out a little bowl of fruit compôte at a time. It's very high in fibre so don't eat too large of a bowl!! It smells really lovely and tastes great!

A Little Note: My husband's mom made this compôte a few days before Christmas and then Christmas morning he remembers enjoying it after all the kids had opened their stockings ... along with a few bites of a chocolate Santa! We made this fruit compôte the first year that we were married. You really could make this anytime of the year!

Enjoy,
Teresa

Ribbon Salad

Gluten Free

1 package Lime JELLO
1 package Lemon JELLO
1 package Raspberry JELLO
3 cups Boiling Water
1 cup Marshmallows, miniature
2 (3 oz) packages Cream Cheese, softened
1 ½ cups Cold Water
½ cup Mayonaise
19 oz can Pineapple, crushed & drained well
½ cup Whipped Cream

Dissolve the three packages of JELLO in three separate bowls. Use 1 cup boiling water for each. Stir each bowl well.

Stir marshmallows into lemon jello and set aside.

Add 3/4 cup cold water to lime jello and pour into 9x13 pan or individual glasses.

Add 3/4 cup cold water to raspberry JELLO, set aside at room temperature.

Add cream cheese to lemon mixture, beat until blended. Chill until slightly thickened. Then, stir in mayonnaise, whipped cream and drained pineapple. Spoon gently over SET lime jello.

Place in fridge to chill.

Chill raspberry JELLO until slightly thick and pour over lemon mixture. Chill until firm. Cut the 9x13 pan into squares and serve.

My husband thinks it's dessert ... but it is salad! My Gramma said so!

A Little Note: As a child, and until I had children of my own, we would gather at my Aunt & Uncles house for Christmas dinner. We had over 30 people that would gather for a feast around that long table, talking, laughing and eating way too much! My Gramma always brought this 'salad' ... I loved it! As a child, I thought it was beautiful and I couldn't believe we could eat jello for supper. As an adult, I always think of my Gramma when I eat this 'salad'. Christmas isn't complete without it!

Enjoy,
Teresa

"Life is either a daring adventure or nothing."
--Helen Keller

Maple Pecan Chicken

Gluten, Dairy & Egg Free

6 Chicken Breasts, cut in half
¼ cup Cornstarch
1 tbsp. Canola or Olive Oil
½ Onion, chopped
1 tsp. Ginger, minced
½ cup Maple Syrup
½ cup Chicken Stock
¼ cup Apple Juice
¼ cup Balsamic Vinegar
1 Fresh Squeezed Mandarin Orange
½ cup Pecans
½ cup Frozen Cranberries

Put the cornstarch and chicken pieces in a sealed ziploc bag and shake.

Heat a fry pan with the oil. Place the coated chicken pieces in a hot fry pan, brown both sides. Remove browned chicken from the pan.

Place pieces in a large casserole dish.

Add a little extra oil to the pan, if the pan doesn't have much oil left in it. Then add the onion and cook for 2-3 minutes, stirring frequently.

Add ginger and stir for 30 seconds.

Then add maple syrup, chicken stock, apple juice, mandarin orange juice and balsamic vinegar to pan. Stir well and let this mixture come to a boil.

Pour mixture over the chicken and cover with a lid or aluminum foil.

Bake for 1 hour in a 375°F oven.

If you are having company, you can prep this recipe earlier in the day and then place the casserole dish in the fridge. From my experience, if you refrigerate this dish, you need to cook it 30-40 minutes longer as it needs time to warm through to the middle.

I love making this dish when we have company because it can be made ahead. Dishes that can be made ahead and allow you to clean up your kitchen and be organized to enjoy your company.

If dinner gets delayed, this recipe is forgiving ... it is no problem to leave it in the oven for a bit longer!

A Little Note: In our household, this dish has become a Christmas seasonal favourite. My 'old' friend gave this recipe to me years ago and since then I have made a few changes.

When you serve this to guests, it looks festive. What I like is that it can be prepped early in the day and it allows you to enjoy more time with your family and friends. All the aromas smell very Christmassy!

Enjoy,
Teresa

"If A is a success in life, then A equals x plus y plus z. Work is x... y is play... and z is keeping your mouth shut."
--Albert Einstein

Turkey Stuffing

Gluten, Dairy & Egg Free

1 ½ to 2 Loaves of Gluten Free Bread - I use Mom's Nutritious Loaf*
2 tbsps. Butter (Dairy Free, if needed)
1 Onion, chopped fine
¼ cup Craisins
¼ cup Raisins
½ cup Dried Apricots, diced
1 Apple, cored & diced
¾ cup Celery, diced
3 cloves Garlic, minced
1 tsp. Rosemary
1 tsp. Thyme
1 tsp. Sage
½ tsp. Salt
½ tsp. Pepper
¾ to 1 cup GF Chicken Stock OR GF Mushroom Soup. I use homemade or Epicures stock. I prefer the taste and texture of stock plus it's dairy free, but others like the mushroom soup. You can decide for your family.

Stuffing can be prepped up to 24 hours ahead of time. Hold back the chicken stock or mushroom soup just prior to stuffing the bird or baking it in a casserole dish.

In a skillet, heat butter over medium heat. Sauté onions, celery and garlic until golden. Approximately 5 minutes.

In a large bowl toss together cubed bread, cooled onion mixture, cranberries, raisins, apricots, apple, herbs, salt & pepper.

Add chicken stock (or mushroom soup) just prior to stuffing the bird or baking it in a casserole dish.

Clean, rinse and pat dry the turkey. Stuff bird with stuffing. Any extra stuffing you have, put it in to a greased casserole dish with a lid or foil.

Place the stuffed turkey into the roasting pan and follow cooking instructions for a turkey, based on the weight of your turkey.

You want to make sure the inside of the bird/stuffing comes to the correct temperature, to avoid food poisoning. Use a thermometer to ensure it has reached proper temperature.

If cooking in a casserole dish, you will need to bake about 45-60 minutes at 400°F. Last 5-10 minutes leave lid off to brown a bit.

Casserole dish baking avoids any food borne illness if you don't cook the turkey long enough, so you choose which you wan to do!

A Little Note: *I use a loaf called 'Mom's Nutritious Loaf' from my online baking classes (link on GFKOB's Facebook page). The loaf is dairy, gluten and egg free and it tastes great in this recipe. If you do not have this recipe or don't have time to bake, you can use a bread of your choice. I have found Northern Bakehouse has turned out well when I don't have time to bake either! I can find it in my local grocery stores or Costco.

We make this recipe for the entire extended family, and everyone likes it!

Enjoy,
Teresa

"Failure is success if we learn from it."
--Malcolm S. Forbes

Lefsa

Gluten, Dairy & Egg Free

3 cups Mashed Potatoes
½ cup Butter (can substitute Dairy Free, if needed)
½ cup My Favourite 1:1 Gluten Free Flour*
1 tsp. xanthan gum*
1 tbsp. Sugar
1 tsp. Salt
½ tsp. Baking Powder

*Flour blend is VERY important in end product. If you decide to use a different flour blend, do NOT add the xanthan gum from this recipe if it has a gum already in it.

Mix all of the ingredients together with a Kitchen-Aid or electric mixer. Separate the dough in half. Roll each half into a log that is about two inches in diameter. Wrap each log with plastic wrap and put into the fridge to chill.

Turn on griddle to bring it to temperature. The temperature is very important for lefsa but each griddle is unique. Therefore it is a bit of trial and error. Start with 375°F and adjust as needed. Then write down the temperature needed for your griddle, for future.

Grab a roll from the fridge. Cut off a slice of dough to roll (a small handful). Place on a well floured pastry mat. Roll dough flat with rolling pin, using plenty of flour on mat and rolling pin. Transfer to hot griddle and cook for approximately 1-2 minutes (should have brown spots), flip over and cook the other side for another 1 minute. Lefsa is cooked when it has brown spots on it. Take the piece of lefsa off the griddle and place on a tea towel. Repeat for remaining dough.

Cool between tea towels. Can be stored in the freezer or fridge.

My Gram kept the lefsa wrapped in tea towels when she stored it. I don't know if the tea towels are necessary ... but I just do it because my Gram said so!

A Little Note: My Gramma made lefsa every Christmas. She had a special lefsa rolling pin and would stand for hours making many batches for her family. Then, on Christmas day, lefsa would be piled on a plate to be enjoyed. The family enjoyed rolling it up with butter and we all sprinkled sugar on the inside. The plate seemed to be filled continually throughout the meal, as my Dad, and all of his brothers, devoured the lefsa. I think I ate more lefsa than anything else on my plate.

When I was diagnosed celiac, I tried to make lefsa and it was a disaster. So, I did not have lefsa for years.

Then, I decided that I had to figure it out, so my kids could enjoy this lovely tradition. I found that the lefsa rolling pin didn't work well with gluten free dough. The dough got stuck in the grooves and was impossible to clean.

Therefore, just use a normal rolling pin and it will taste great. You will only be missing the markings .. but still enjoy the tradition! I hope you enjoy my Gram's lefsa recipe … gluten free style!

Enjoy,
Teresa

"You see, in life, lots of people know what to do, but few people actually do what they know. Knowing is not enough! You must take action."
--Anthony Robbins

Cinnamon Buns

Gluten Dairy & Egg Free

1 ½ cups Brown Rice Flour
½ cup White Rice Flour
½ cup Tapioca Starch
¼ cup Potato Starch
½ tsp. Salt
1 tsp. Baking Powder
1 Flax Egg (1 tbsp. ground flax & 2 tbsps. water)
1 tbsp. Instant Yeast
½ tbsp. Honey
½ tbsp. Maple Syrup
2 tbsps. Olive Oil
2 cups Warm Water
½ cup Ground Chia
¼ cup WHOLE Psyllium Husk
¼ cup Butter or Coconut Oil (if dairy free)
½ cup Brown Sugar
3 tbsps. Cinnamon

GLAZE
1 cup Icing Sugar
2 to 3 tbsps. Milk of Choice

In a small dish, combine the "flax egg" (water and ground flax) and set to the side. Or you can use an egg, if you choose.

In your mixing bowl place the warm water, yeast, maple syrup and honey. Stir gently and let it sit.

In a separate bowl stir your flours, starches, salt and baking powder. Set to the side.

Add your oil, flax egg, ground chia and psyllium husk to the water mixture, stir quickly to combine. Let it sit for 1 minute and stir again. Pour the dry ingredients into the mixing bowl with the water mixture. Mix on low until combined and then increase the speed to medium. Mix for 3 minutes.

Roll out the dough into a rectangle that is approximately 12"x16" in size. You can use a bit of brown rice flour if the dough is a bit sticky, but you won't need much. Pour melted butter or coconut oil evenly onto the dough, then evenly spread the brown sugar and cinnamon on top.

Roll the dough into a 'log' and cut into pieces, about 1 inch each. Separate the pieces you have cut and you will have circles. Place the circles into a greased pie plate. If you have extra, bake them in a muffin tin.

Let the plate of cinnamon buns rise for 25 minutes.

Bake at 400°F for 20-25 minutes.

Mix the glaze together in a small bowl. Drizzle glaze over the warm cinnamon buns.

Buns taste great warm!

A Little Note: These are absolutely tasty! They have great texture and are the best cinnamon buns that I have eaten since being diagnosed celiac. Waking up Christmas morning to warm cinnamon buns is a pretty nice treat. You can make them the night before and put them into the fridge covered, then get up early in the morning to let them warm up on the counter before baking. They turn out best making them the same day.

Enjoy,
Teresa

"The path to success is to take massive, determined action."
--Anthony Robbins

Another Great Recipe: _____

Ingredients: *Directions:*

Tips:

Another Great Recipe: _____

Ingredients: *Directions:*

_____ _____
_____ _____
_____ _____
_____ _____
_____ _____
_____ _____
_____ _____
_____ _____
_____ _____
_____ _____
_____ _____
_____ _____
_____ _____
_____ _____
_____ _____
_____ _____
_____ _____
_____ _____
_____ _____
_____ _____
_____ _____
_____ _____

Tips:

_____
_____
_____
_____

Notes

Notes

Index of Recipes by Category

Cookies
Chewy Gingersnap Cookies - Gluten & Dairy Free   15
Crescent Shortbread - Gluten Free   17
Gingerbread House & Gingerbread Men - Gluten & Dairy Free   23
Great Gramma Swansons Shortbread - Gluten Free   22
Royal Icing for Gingerbread House - Gluten & Dairy Free   25
Royal Icing for Sugar Cookies - Gluten & Dairy Free   20
Sugar Cookies - Gluten & Dairy Free   18
Whipped Shortbread - Gluten & Egg Free   27

Squares
Chocolate Dreams - Gluten Free   33
Date Squares - Gluten, Dairy & Egg Free   39
Nanaimo Bars - Gluten Free   35
Pineapple Squares - Gluten & Dairy Free   41
Toffee Bars - Gluten & Egg Free   37

Desserts
Butter Tart Filling - Gluten Free   47
Pie Dough - Gluten & Dairy Free   50
Pumpkin Pie Filling - Gluten Free   48
Sticky Toffee Pudding - Gluten Free   52
Trifle - Gluten Free   54

Miscellaneous Recipes
Boxing Day Dip - Gluten Free   61
Chex Mix - Nut and Bolts - Gluten & Dairy Free   63
Cinnamon Buns - Gluten Dairy & Egg Free   75
Fruit Compôte - Gluten, Dairy & Egg Free   66
Lefsa - Gluten, Dairy & Egg Free   73
Maple Pecan Chicken - Gluten, Dairy & Egg Free   69
My Favourite 1:1 Gluten Free Flour - Gluten, Dairy & Egg Free   62
Ribbon Salad - Gluten Free   67
Sweet Potatoes - Gluten, Dairy & Egg Free   64
Turkey Stuffing - Gluten, Dairy & Egg Free   71

www.ingramcontent.com/pod-product-compliance
Lightning Source LLC
Chambersburg PA
CBHW040159100526
44590CB00001B/9